THIS ROCKING MOTION OF TIME

poems by

Yvonne Pearson

Finishing Line Press
Georgetown, Kentucky

THIS ROCKING MOTION
OF TIME

ACKNOWLEDGMENTS

Anatomy of a Quarrel, Studio One; Reprinted in *The Crisp Pine*
One for Each Hand, *Writers' Journal*
Early Treatment Could Save Your Life, *Sidewalks*
Eaten Alive, *Literary Mama*
Autobiography of Births, *Main Street Rag*
Respite; Memory Care Unit, *St. Paul Almanac*
Common Prayer; Close Up, *Open to Interpretation: Fading Light*
Crossing the Continental Divide, *Crossing Lines Anthology*
In the Eye of the Beholder, *Split Rock Review*
How Fast the Body; Log Cabin; Graduation Ritual, under different title (June
Ritual); Farm Summer, *Talking Stick*
Poaching, *Waters Deep: A Great Lakes Poetry Anthology*
Funeral, *Plainsong*
Waiting for Test Results, *Courtship of Winds*

Publisher: Leah Huete de Maines
Editor: Christen Kincaid
Cover Art: Yvonne Pearson
Author Photo: Carl Pearson
Cover Design: Elizabeth Maines McCleavy

Order online: www.finishinglinepress.com
also available on amazon.com

Author inquiries and mail orders:
Finishing Line Press
PO Box 1626
Georgetown, Kentucky 40324
USA

Table of Contents

POACHING

Late April, sliver of moon.
We hiked the lazy dirt road,
not yet rippled by washboards
carved in the dry dirt of July.
We brought spears to nail silver flashes
of Northerns spawning in the creek.
This land belonged to us.
Just out of mud season,
moisture scented everything,
poplar trees, sprinkle of maples, us,
drunk on the smell of new leaves.
We were dark shapes to each other,
and sharp whispers.
That was enough.

Pebbles crunched under our feet.
On lucky nights we could hear the coyotes
calling in the distance.
This was the way of our fathers
when they were young.
Carrying flashlights,
on the lookout for game wardens,
ready to douse the flame.
Money was scarce;
we needed free venison, free fish,
ducks and geese.
And who were city folks anyway to tell us
when and how to catch our game?

Today, the creek is channeled
through a concrete culvert.
The dirt road still meanders,
but higher and wider,
no longer gutted by spring's mud holes.
Some nights there are still whispers under the moon.
The pesky washboards remain,
stubborn, born naturally of the tension
between tires and dry heat.

FARM SUMMER

The day we mounted the horse—
      —princess—
a tall and haunchy female,
I clung to you, my own
powerful female,
as princess carried us
down the hill and into the pasture
to claim the cattle for milking.
She plunged into the shallow creek
and sunk her fine-spun legs
deep in mud. Deep
in mud. My heart fluttered
as the horse bucked and pulled.
Princess heaved herself, and us, free,
and we galloped up the hill
calling come boss
come boss. The reins laid lightly
against the agile neck
turned the horse left and right
through bristled pines.
The cattle lowed and then turned,
slowly as flowers closing for the night,
and lumbered toward the barn
where my uncle would lean his head
against each hot haunch in turn
and pull the milk, frothing white,
into pail after pail.

SCHOOL BUS DRIVER

When the snows swirled
in the narrowings and caught
the wheels in drifts solid as concrete,
the children were glad.
The driver worried the wheels
back and forth
    back and forth
  back,
hoisted his body,
    hoisted his body from the seat,
descended the stairs and stared,
pulled out a shovel and,
with the thin aluminum shell,
sliced blocks of snow.
The children didn't see
how the weight bent my father's back,
how the worry drew wrinkles
on his cheeks.

When the rains softened
the ground, created pools
of clay without bottom
that trapped the wheels,
the children were glad.
The driver gunned the engine
rocked the old yellow bus
back and forth
    back and forth
  back,
hoisted his body,
    hoisted his body from the seat,
descended the stairs and stared,
fetched sticks from beyond the ditch
to fit under the wheels.
The children didn't see
how the pressure cracked
my father's back, how it
scraped his spirit thin.

A road made of dirt
is changed

by rain, wind, snow,
by fingers and toes,
by intention.
A dry August molded the road
into ripples, brittle and waiting
for the bus to begin its rounds
in the fall. A taunting girl crooked
an index finger and scratched
holes in the road,
one in the middle here,
one on the west side there,
another closer to the edge,
a doublewide further down the middle,
"so your dad will get stuck."
Not yet old enough to know better,
I followed behind her, repacking
each depression with dirt,
already knowing he needed me.

EARLY TREATMENT COULD SAVE YOUR LIFE

I found the article in the outhouse,
the summer I was twelve.
The crusted building far from the house
where the graveyard now lies,
wood slab with a hole in the center,
creaky floor where a garden snake
surprised me at dusk.
Redbook Magazine, pages
glommed together like old pasta
from endless leaky days.

"Early Warning Signs of Cancer:
1. A lump in your breast.
See a doctor immediately."
My breasts were new then,
white flour pancakes rising
to a bubble off my chest
and full of tender lumps.
So when Jimmy asked me
to go rollerskating, I knew
I had better do it. I'd be dead
the summer after for sure.

That was the same summer
the Second Coming almost
killed me. We stood in a line
—mom, dad, brothers, sisters, me—
gaping at the August sky,
shafts of colored light
lurching in the northern half.
Mom in ecstasy. The lights
were trees crashing in a wind
storm, and the world
was about to end.

I've built my own outhouse now,
a shingled building not too far
from the cabin, a wood slab
with a hole in the center, the
New Yorker to keep us company.
and when I lie in the meadow

and the northern lights spill down the sky,
I close my eyes and repeat to myself,
I do not have cancer
It is not the Second Coming.

SIXTEEN

I peel garden brown potatoes at 4:30.
Supper 5:30 sharp.
Drop the peels into a plastic pail.
Add water. Slop.
Slop the pigs.

Dump the pail on the pigs' heads.
They snort and shove under falling peels,
reckless of the cold splash on my bare legs.

Barefoot in my short shorts
with three bumblebees sewn on the ass.
Mud puddling between my toes.

My yearning still nameless,
sharp and prickling
as the hairs on their bristled backs.

WHITE SHEETS

Field of pure white
solace for the eye,
          sunlight
reflected off snow,
speckless,
sparkling
clean as Everest.

We brought such color—
tawny skin, red ripe lips,
the chestnut patch
between your legs—
found the rainbow hidden
in the white.

How did we dare
drop into that sunlit-blinded place?
The immaculate we longed for,
the cleansed and elegant field
we were compelled to risk.

All that's left to prove
our presence
are these nuances
of texture left behind,
the rutted shapes of moguls,
scoops and swirls,
hills and hummocks,
a snow field's sign
of breathless work and pleasure.

ANATOMY OF A QUARREL

I.

Our shouts ricochet
off the walls of the room
we usually reserve
for evening reading—
    you always
 you did
 you can't
—bullets aimed well
at the soft organs.
Across the hall we hear
children stirring dreams;
and so reminded of
the garden we are growing
together, we soften the words
we hurl across the couch.
Your eyes water,
my stomach twists,
we cannot hold our fire.

II.

I trudge
a winter
sidewalk,
clenching
my teeth
around our
fight, my
breath sour
from words
I have hidden
under my tongue.

The chill trail
of anger yawning
before me

clamps shut
its icy jaw
and drags
me along.

III.

My mind, an ice floe,
scrapes old debris
across the days,
caught in the chill
of its rigid mold.
Until
the warmth of your voice overheard
as you change the baby's diaper,
the warmth of your voice remembered
when you whispered in our bed,
begins piece by piece
to thaw the frozen trap.

IV.

When we sit once again
In our reading room
talking of what summer
will bring,
I return to our
human garden,
to you, the
bloodroot
from which the
seeds have come,
sink my toes
in the black loam,
watch you, too,
bare your feet, the
scent of cinnamon
and basil in the air.

LOVE POEMS TO MY INFANT DAUGHTER

1. You stroke my cheek
My finger slides
Down ivory side
To rose bud feet
We are lovers
At night when
The world is still and
No one calls to me
You and I return
To one flesh, fused
You beg my breast
Mouths and bellies
Arms and thighs
We circle
The earth

2. My crossed legs form a cradle
where you lie in languid pleasure
taking slippery snacks with your tongue.
Drunk on my body's food
you fall back in milken stupor
chanting ma-ma-ma-ma-ma-ma-ma-ma-mam.

THE COMMON PRAYER

The girl cannot stay in her bed.
Jesus requires of her one more prayer.

> *...if I die before I wake*
> *I pray the Lord my soul to take...*

The covers are warm but
she must go back to her knees

> *... and Jesus will come*
> *like a thief in the night...*

will take her mother, leave her behind
unless she gets back to her knees

> *....Please Jesus....*
> *I want to be born again...*

her knees are getting so cold.

My children never say I pray
the Lord my soul to take.
God knows I don't want him
to take their souls
or their wolf-cub bodies.
I work voodoo on my knees
beside their beds.
Jesus Christ, my husband says,
won't you ever come to bed?

Night falls on my babies.
My girl dreams she's lost me

> *.... and the sins*
> *shall be visited...*

I blow lightly on her face,
stroke her cheek, cross her wrists
hoping Jesus can't get past
the sign of the cross.

ONE FOR EACH HAND

I pull a yellow blanket
under my daughter's chin,
stand back to consider:
she was obnoxious today;
I love her.
One thought for each hand.
I hold them together.

This day I stop
breaking her into parts.
I have kept the brown eyes,
the pirouettes, like some Juliette,
hands held limp at the wrist,
cracked off the tantrum following;
I have kept her words,
well-formed, big as ambition,
broken off the rude ones; and
in the cracking killed.

This day I stop
breaking her into parts.
As Love does, I will
gather her whole
in two hands together.

EATEN ALIVE

Hamburgers
Carrots
Milk
Apples
Bananas
Peanut butter
Orange juice...
They're always hungry.
All day I feed and I feed.
I know why the sow
devours her young.
But it would stop
the driven mother
at the trough
if only piglets
could learn
to pronounce
her name.

BEDTIME DANCE

At half past eight the bedtime clock
chimes the beat for Charlie's dance—
A two-step, swing,
A swoop, he clings,
I sling him back.
A waddle, waltz,
his start is false,
I catch him fast,
cast him back.
Bee-bop, ballet,
Breakaway!
I'll nab you yet,
you little guy!

At last—
A pas de deux.
His feet slow down,
our steps in sync.
A slide, a glide,
we coast toward bed.
Dance master
now, I fold him
under covers.
Leave him
lost in lullabies,
his private melodies.

FREEDOM

And there rises in me
this image of Emily
stalking on her toddler legs
across the long lawn
at grandma's house
where she pushes through
the final spears of grass,
the ones that got away
from the mower, until she stands
on the tufts of lawn at the
sandy edge of the lake.
With no thought of caution,
consequences, alternatives,
she leaps up, thrusts both legs
straight out in front of her,
and lands on her merry buttocks,
shouting *blast off* all the way down.

BIRD WATCHING

The music the little boy sings
lololololololololo
as he tries to form words
about stones and bees
and the neighbor's cat

lololololololololo
he trills as he tries
to speak his joy
for the larkspur
for the front stoop
for the paint-peeled stair
that leads down
from his own red door

his descent on the steps
disrupted by one foot set
too close to the other,
he falls from the last step
short his goal: a stick, the
snapped wing of a maple.

Low now in the trenches
he howls at injustice
at skinned knees and empty bellies
all around the world, and
the sparrow sings to him

Morning has broken

So he unfolds like a crane
sings lolololololololo
to the sparrow
alight in the oak
on the boulevard
who has been waiting for him
to join in the melodies
that shape the world.

RESPITE

Skin flakes like the brown earth.
The grass, each small and singular
strand, lies listless, without hope.
The squirrels, rulers
of the urban wood, sit and stare.
Even the lilac languishes,
brief glorious scent threatened.
Machined air hums in the houses.
On the sidewalks
there are no mothers watching
there are no children playing.
We are shut-ins against the heat.

So when the rain comes,
pelting hard like in the old days,
my kids run into the street to
build a dam, a big dam, and I don't care.
They haul wet pine needles
and old grass to the gutter.
Piles of it. And the water
backs up. It bubbles balloon scraps,
twigs, a rough catch in a willow branch.
Rain flattens grass to ground,
hair to cheeks, and though
its getting dark
I do not call them in.

MORNING RAIN

Morning rain hangs water drops glowing
with sun on the clothesline. I wonder,
when Russia's Chernobyl nuclear plant melted down,
did their raindrops glow with radiation?
How much time does it take for the earth to heal?
I clip up tiny blue overalls, a daisy-painted skirt,
white dress shirts, a 50/50 cotton blend.
This palette of our lives.
I have photographed so many clotheslines—
turquoise towels and jewel dresses in Tortola,
brick red sheets and brown trousers in Bedouin backyards,
sundresses and bikinis floating on lines in Florida—
so many hopeful lives.
I clip up the lavender dress my girl wore
when we thought we'd lost her,
dropped off on the wrong side of town by the school bus driver.
We come back from these things, heal, mostly,
and there hang the blue stretch pants she wears now.
There hangs the receiving blanket
for the third child swelling my belly,
and the flowered sheet, the one that held our wet, loving bodies when
we bet on the future, bet against unnatural rain,
bet on the clothesline that there would always be
time for healing.

FUNERAL

The marigolds are indiscriminate,
a profusion plying roadside
and garden alike. They take no notice.
The sky is perfect blue,
cerulean joy demanding more
than its share of the scene.
The mother is a wooden toy,
her arms stretched into straight pins
as she falls against the coffin,
her head bent back,
her gaunt face exposed.
She would have the sky take her,
carry her away in mare's tail clouds,
a gauze of torn strips.

LOG CABIN

At dusk the cabin's fire warms us
as coyotes howl, phonics of the wild,
the pack singing to the whitened night.

The full moon washes our log walls,
trees that gave their backs to my husband's adze,
their white flesh glistening with sap like sweat

in the summer sun, balanced one on another,
pinned with 80-penny nails, walls that have
curbed and contained our wanderlust.

Inside these walls we have lain
three dolls, asleep in a row in the loft.
Only we are not playing at this.

They are breakable, these young ones.
Their breaths play a symphony of syncopation,
each marking a beat that says *I live*.

We fall asleep to the sound of the wind
brushing the branch of the poplar against
the roof, its cedar shakes keeping us dry.

WATCHING MY GIRL DANCE

What is it that hides there
in the dance?
Yes, you see it.
Curled—there—
where his leg presses against hers.
Do you see it stirring as they move?

--There—
it slides up the thin space
between their shoulders,
a long thin question mark.
And now--
   --ahhh—

it plays in the space
where his hands are, there
where he lifts her hips above his head.

Is this love? The bodies
yearning for each other?
for resolution?
Or is it the breath
of the cumulus cloud calling?

Is it the hot breath that first created them
and creates them again as they fall,
wind-blown petals,
into each other's arms?

HOW FAST THE BODY

The rain swooped in
on wings as white as hyacinths
flew in from the East and nested
in feathered palms.

It had gathered
in a portent flock on the horizon
burst suddenly, and in a frenzied wish
rushed headlong down where

I was floating,
waiting for the wisdom of water

marveling at the dolphin body
of my daughter
at how fast the body arches,
soon ready for deeper seas.

How do we live with
this rocking motion of time?

The drops swooped in
with no answers, only
the soft beat on the bed
of the sea, empty,
whispers without words,
kisses breaking on my cheeks.

GRADUATION OPEN HOUSE

The lace of lilacs tumbles
from the crystal vase.
Every spring
I bring this fleeting bounty
to my bedroom.
The flower of brides.

This year I bring
the entire tree inside,
fill my house with
lavender lilacs
purple lilacs
lilac scent
cascading from piano,
table, glass, and tile,
more fragile than lilies
more fleeting than roses.
The flower of babies
and old women.
I fill my house today
with riotous beauty,
lilac bursting open the season.

It's the day we celebrate her leave taking.
We lay out strawberries, cream cheese, watermelon, wine.
We lay out stories, paintings, and old photos:
one of my belly swelling welcome
under cotton flowers, me still sole owner of the girl;
one of her tulip head cradled in her father's palm;
one of our girl feeding her baby brother;
our girl naked under the walnut tree. Slowly the scenes change.
She preens for the first dancing party,
hugs friends, climbs the Grand Canyon,
builds habitat houses;
she's wrapped in lavender chiffon and white prom roses.

We lay out toffee cookies and tea ring,
we lay out brownies and welcome
to a hundred people who cannot help us
as we lay out our swelling godspeed hearts
and I bring lilacs to her bedside table,

A first bouquet for her,
the fragrance filling the room
she prepares to leave.

CASSATT'S MATERNAL CARESS, 1891
In the Museum of Fine Arts, Boston

It's rose—no, not quite—it's salmon
colored on the chair, the carpet,
papered on the wall. She let
in petal colors only, common.

Placed just so in the chair
pink flesh, gray silk, juxtaposed,
give contrast, gentle, almost
like a prayer, but I care

not at all about the room,
just about the child pressed
against her cheek. Crest
of a new moon. He will not ruin

spotless white of goose down
on the bed. He is content
to dwell in happiness,
stops right there. As silk gown

serves the chair, her face
is counterpoint to his.
Something's amiss.
Her eyes disrupt the painted grace.

Of course she knows. At birth, abrupt,
the awful aching grows.
The same a hundred years ago.
She knows that even as she cups

the naked child, the moment
she would own moves past.

BROKEN WING

On the other side of the glass
snow falls and falls, and though
it is glittering, ermined,
has drained the world of color.

The phone pulses. His voice:
It's your right to know, but
I don't want to talk about it.
I'm okay. Don't worry.

He's always been our quiet one,
a core of caution camouflaged
by desperate risks. My boy's voice

quavers when he calls me back:
I'm okay. Don't you worry,
and I wait as he reaches for the breath
that will hold him to this world,
my fingernails gripped in my fist.
Worry is the birthright
of a mother. If only I could
prism this snow-white world
into a rainbow of promise. Once

he found a bird with broken wing,
carried it carefully in the palm
of his hand as if his hand were a hospital
bed sheathed in soft silks,
lined a shoe box with tissues
and tender leaves
for the starling's convalescence,
brought it worms from the black dirt
in the back yard. I yearn for him now
to give to himself the tender care
he once gave to a bird.

I think of his joy the day
when we gave the bird back to the world,
when we gave the world back to the bird.

AN AUTOBIOGRAPHY OF BIRTHS

I was born on Flag Day, 1947. Born Again at Bible Camp
      on the Fourth of July, 1955. Again and again, actually—
on my knees in the pink room under the twilight sun, and before
      I was baptized in the murky waters of Spoon Lake, and after
Martin fell off the ladder, until Memorial Day 1969, when I left
      Bible College, the year the Cossack showed me I could get heaven
on earth. Memorial Day, 1970, I began my search for another birth. Rolf
      in Germany, Jack in Spain, Hans in Holland, Terry at Bruge.
Home for Labor Day, and Jenny next door had gotten born again. Oscar
      woke from a dream so horny he spun his cock like a top, and
Nixon bombed the hell out of Viet Nam. Thanksgiving, moved to
      Washington, ran with a thousand long-haired flower children in
the Capitol streets, and I didn't care if Oscar was horny or Jenny believed.
      I have eaten berries with the Chief Justice of the Supreme Court,
ridden motorcycles weed-high on wet streets, made love on the exposed
      side of the Spanish Sierras, seen the children's drawings of bombs
and people dropping from the Laotian sky, witnessed Chuck Colson's
      being born again. I have given birth, once, and again, and once
again, nursed my babies while watching famine on television, watched
      babies die, not mine, watched babies taken away for not being fed,
or being broken, for being whipped, babies discarded. I have watched
      a child buried under the bloom of iris, and still I harbor hope
for other births. I want to be born again and again to blossoms and onions,
      to children straining at the halyards, full jib to the wind,
to my own weathered hull.

MEMORY CARE UNIT

Words don't mean much here.
Take Ida, who is excited to hear:
there is a phone call for her!
She turns to the window
to pick up her glasses.
The message is repeated,
a phone call for you Ida,
and she is excited to hear:
there is a phone call for her!

Allen speaks in Russian,
Jim answers in Greek,
the conversation pleasing
to both partners, who nod and laugh.
The old, mostly women,
spoon mashed potatoes and stare,
or talk randomly...I want...honey...
oh my...pillow...pretty horses...
nice...pudding... words strung
randomly like disrupted DNA.

My mother greets me with a rippling giggle.
Inked on her parchment palm the name
of her new man, her sweet guy.
She curls her fingers into a fist so
she can hold on to him. We walk
the path behind the building admiring
the child—my grandson, her great—
and she wonders if it was hard for me
to give birth to him. Not at all, I say,
which, I reason, is true in the most literal way.

I won't tire her with irrelevance; after all,
we don't rebuke the tulip when its petals fall.
I've given up on words. We sit together,
her head on my shoulder, my cheek resting
on her hair and let the sun set.

CLOSE UP

Like a print creased from age,
flecks falling from the cracks,
we lost parts of her,

faded
a year at a time
a month at a time
a day at a time.

Some would have it
that a painting
is more true to reality
than is a photograph,
that it captures
a vibrancy,
a character,
a photo cannot.

I would argue
a photograph
is more true to reality,
no matter how
well-cared for,
with age
a photo fades,
loses its acuity
and color.

SEPARATION

She lies on her side
in a bed
in the dark
in the scent
of ointment and pudding.
Her arms lift,
climb
an invisible rope.
She rocks
side to side.
Her throat rumbles
with wordless sound,
her ready giggle
garbled and gone.
Dying is such
hard work.

After three days
her eyes are caved,
her knees rubbed red
from the circles
she's scribed with her legs.
Does she know
we are here?
Does she know
I lie
by her side?
She is quiet now,
and we watch
her pulse flutter
in the hollow
of her collar bone,
until it lays down
its burden.

I reach for
the warmth
that lingers
in the hollow
of her arm.

DISCONNECTING LIFE SUPPORT FOR MY FATHER-IN-LAW

His breath rattles through the Christmas season
like castanets shaking out of rhythm.
His son, still longing, reaches
for the hands, callused, fisted.
The geranium withers on the windowsill.

   We're waiting for someone to make a decision.

Silence vaults the room, green visions flicker
on the heart monitor, doctors slide whitely by,
penicillin, lithium the sacraments.
It's dark and the doctors whisper. I long for lights
blinking on the balsam tree across town.
His son longs for light in the eyes.

   We're waiting for someone to make a decision.

A cheek twitches, a hand jerks. Bring wires.
Quickly. The brain stem needs re-connecting.
Remember the convoluted gray brain-on-a-shelf
in the biology classroom. Turn it upside down.
Study it now. Help him.

   We're waiting for someone....

The jowls are flaccid. No smiles to pull them up.
No anger to set them hard. Bring something.
His cheeks need air.

   We're waiting....

Give us something here. A clap in the breach,
a curtain split for a moment, a glimpse of lightening.
Where is the arc of electricity that makes a path for us?
Isn't this where we are supposed to meet God?

   Waiting....

CROSSING THE CONTINENTAL DIVIDE

Here at the crest of the hill
affinities surrender
snow scatters, water sheds
east and west, rivers diverge
from each other.

Here at the crest of the hill
Think how things divide—
The bark from the birch,
The peach from the tree,
The earth at its fault lines.

Think how things divide—
The messy split of egg from shell,
Here from *after*, *no* from *where*,
And babies from their mothers.
Sand from sea, salt from water,
You from me.

We climb the hill to watch,
And wish against all evidence.
Join *be* to *loved, our* to *selves,*
and take more sand to the sea.
We leap fault lines,

even knowing someday
Life and *time* will diverge.
Time will sunder rock
from mountains. *For* and
ever cannot stay together.

IN THE EYE OF THE BEHOLDER

This path of tree ferns, regal fronds,
reach fondly for each other,
their beauty lush, careless
of what they shelter:
Berkeley's magnolia blossoms
a doe and her yearling
Steller's jay searching a mate
and us, lurching toward something new,
some beauty that has escaped us all these years.

We waken to the beautiful path and remember
the tree ferns in their native New Zealand,
or Haleakala perfected by protea,
whose spiked fingers curved
in cacophonous colors,
remember Sedona sunsets rouged by red rocks,
or the peculiar beauty of tidal pools, sluiced
with green moss and studded with starfish and urchins,
remember when we were limber and lithe
as the wild ponies on Assateague,
filled with the beauty of possibility.

Look now
your body and mine
creased by years of living
and sheltered by the fronds of the tree ferns,
your elegant hands studded with age spots,
my arms with pockets of skin.
See now this kind of beauty.

WAITING FOR TEST RESULTS

Last time, I lost my mind.

I found it sitting in a pine tree outside
my bedroom. It took a long time
                  to call it back inside.

It's not so tough this time.
   I'm older.

I'm not so scared of dying
              anymore
                         maybe.

Reality is in constant motion.
I didn't know that before.

The magnolia is loaded with purple hands,
billowed bowls, beautiful urns.

More nouns
         are lost
   every day.

There are days I long to live
                  inside a magnolia blossom.

BELLY UP

To lie belly up with one's arms wide open,
vulnerable as Christ on the cross—

Light enters through the soft skin
that covers the belly and breast.
As light does.

 I cannot choose what comes in,
 The darkened line, the shadow
enters with the light? So be it.

The way you draw the line makes all the difference.
A thick line, or a thin line, a line that carries motion,
it's all in the flick of the wrist,
            and my wrist
will remain gently flexed in a gesture of welcome.

www.ingramcontent.com/pod-product-compliance
Lightning Source LLC
Chambersburg PA
CBHW030500100426
42813CB00002B/284